IMAGES
of America

HILLSBORO

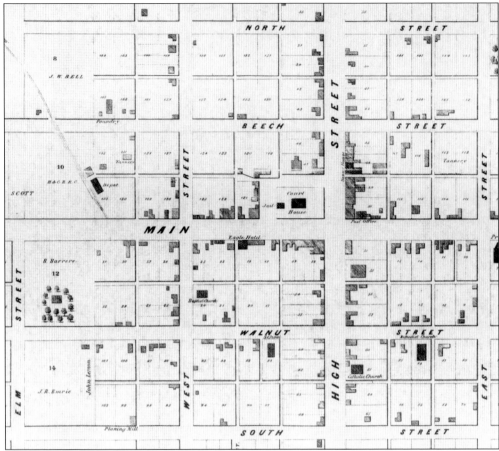

This map of the business district of Hillsboro was made in 1853 by surveyors Manfred & Simpson. The town's layout is simple, with Main and High Streets intersecting in the center of town and East, West, North, and South Streets forming a perimeter. In actual use, however, road names like North East Street and East North Street can be a bit confusing. (Courtesy of the Highland County Historical Society.)

ON THE COVER: Harry "Fat" Wilson, shown here in May 1923, opened the Palms Restaurant in the first floor of Bell's Opera House soon after he graduated from high school in 1919. Wilson was always quick with a smile and a joke and often dressed as Santa during the holidays. He was the uncle and second father of longtime Methodist church organist Clifford Smith. (Courtesy of the Highland County Historical Society.)

IMAGES
of America

HILLSBORO

Tara Beery

ARCADIA
PUBLISHING

Copyright © 2024 by Tara Beery
ISBN 978-1-4671-6086-5

Published by Arcadia Publishing
Charleston, South Carolina

Printed in the United States of America

Library of Congress Control Number: 2023942402

For all general information, please contact Arcadia Publishing:
Telephone 843-853-2070
Fax 843-853-0044
E-mail sales@arcadiapublishing.com

Visit us on the Internet at www.arcadiapublishing.com

To Jeff, Jeffrey, and Mary

CONTENTS

ACKNOWLEDGMENTS

A great debt is owed to the historians and photographers who have preserved so much of Hillsboro's story. These include John Sayler, who took the pictures of the Temperance Crusade in the 1870s; Daniel Scott, who recorded the earliest history of Highland County; and Robert M. Ditty, Charles Collins, and Kirby Smith, who rescued Scott's notes and published his work. In more modern times, there was the illustrious Elsie Ayres, who put together 2,000 pages of history in her two comprehensive books about Highland County. It is amazing how useful and all-encompassing these histories are considering the limited paper record and personal interviews she had to work with. Violet Morgan and Jean Wallis also greatly contributed to the effort to share Hillsboro's history.

Many others have worked hard within the Highland County Historical Society to preserve our heritage. These include all past, present, and future members; the society's hardworking volunteers; those who have donated items to the Highland House Museum; and all who carefully preserve items of local history in private collections. Vicki Knauff, John Glaze, Jim Rooney, and Carolyn Hastings deserve special mention for their tireless efforts to preserve items of local importance that were essential to the creation of this book.

I also wish to thank my father, Lowell Chambers, for putting me to work at his auctions from an early age. It was those many hours of handling antiques at estate sales that sparked my interest in Hillsboro history. Finally, a big thank you to everyone at Arcadia Publishing, especially my editor, Amy Jarvis, for making this book possible.

Unless otherwise noted, all images in this volume appear courtesy of the Highland County Historical Society.

INTRODUCTION

Before the American Revolution, the State of Virginia laid claim to all the land that eventually became Ohio. To encourage men to join the revolt against England, enlistees were promised grants of this Ohio land once the war was won. After the war, some grantees moved to their land, while others sold their claims to land speculators or other settlers.

Highland County was established on February 18, 1805, out of this Virginia Military District. Initially, the county seat was in the town of New Market, and the first basic government offices were set up there. The Ohio General Assembly appointed David Hayes to select a site for the permanent county seat. He made his choice based on its central location and because he surveyed it as the highest point in the county. The town was given the name Hillsborough, probably due to the rolling hills it was laid out on, but some early settlers claimed it was named in honor of Capt. William Hill. Regardless, a federal post office decree in 1891 shortened the name to Hillsboro.

Hayes purchased the original 200 acres that made up Hillsboro from Baltimore land speculator Benjamin Ellicott for $100. Hayes then created a well-thought-out plat for the new city. The two principal streets were Main Street (US Route 50), which travels from the Atlantic Ocean in Maryland to near the Pacific Ocean in California, and High Street (US Route 62), which goes from the Mexican border in Texas to the Canadian border in Niagara Falls, New York. Hayes made these main roads a generous 99 feet wide, while the town's other streets were 66 feet wide.

The first town lots were auctioned off in October 1807, and prices ranged from $20 to $150, with terms of no money down and 12 months to pay. Hayes would no doubt have continued to play a big role in the formation of the new town, but he died in a horrifying accident while engaged in a good-natured horse race soon after the auction.

Hillsboro was an attractive location for new arrivals. It had an unusually healthy environment, which contrasted favorably with the mosquito- and disease-ridden cities of Chillicothe and Cincinnati. Once cleared of thick forests, the surrounding farmland proved to be exceptionally bountiful, and many springs, creeks, and wells provided an abundance of water. The town was also blessed with an unusual number of accomplished citizens who devoted much time and treasure to build strong businesses, good schools, and other civic improvements. One especially prominent citizen, Allen Trimble, served as Ohio's governor in 1822 and again from 1826 to 1830, and the town had a number of other men who were elected to state and federal offices during its early years.

The engaged citizens of Hillsboro considered education to be a priority. Prior to 1825, the town's schools were private affairs, with parents paying a subscription fee for their children to attend. After the State of Ohio created public schools (under a plan started by Governor Trimble), Hillsboro wasted no time in converting the main private school into a public entity. Special care was taken to approve only the very best teachers for the district, ensuring a top-level education was offered by the town.

Early Hillsboro residents were not satisfied with merely offering an excellent basic education. Many concerned parties worked to establish secondary schools. The Hillsboro Academy was the first high school in southern Ohio. Established in 1827, just 20 years after the town was created out of a wilderness, this school prepared young men to attend college. A little over a decade later, in 1839, Hillsboro's first women's college, the Oakland Female Seminary, opened. While this was not the first college in Ohio to permit female students, it was possibly the first to be created specifically to educate young ladies. For the next 60 years, there was at least one—and, for almost a decade, as many as three—college-level institute for female higher education. The students at these schools attained an education equal to that of the college-educated men of the era. This meant that for most of the town's history, the women of Hillsboro had more educational opportunities and were overall better educated than their male peers.

This educational divide made for a more independent female population, and in the 1870s, they seized control of a controversial issue when they launched the Temperance Crusade. These ladies marched on the businesses of all the liquor sellers in town and demanded they close down. Their efforts led directly to the formation of the Women's Christian Temperance Union and the passage of national Prohibition in 1919.

Hillsboro also benefitted from being home to many astute businessmen. The historic business district is small and consists mostly of a two-block stretch of High Street and a two-block stretch of Main Street. Many businesses were crammed into this area, with most buildings containing more than one business. Professionals, such as doctors and lawyers, had their offices mostly on the upper floors, while retail establishments utilized the first floor. There were even businesses in the basements of some buildings. A number of companies thrived for many decades, such as Jacob Sayler's jewelry store, Hibben Dry Goods, and Smith/Ayres drugstore. The C.S. Bell Company lasted for three generations. This foundry produced many different items but is best known for its farm, school, and church bells. Thousands of these bells were sold, and they can still be found all over the world. However, most Hillsboro businesses were much shorter-term enterprises. Partnerships formed and dissolved with startling frequency, and stores often moved physical locations multiple times, which can make it a challenging endeavor to trace the history of a particular company.

The business atmosphere of Hillsboro was supported by the town's auspicious location. A number of state routes and federal highways radiate from Hillsboro like spokes of a bicycle tire, and it is nearly equidistant from Cincinnati, Columbus, and Dayton, so the town had relatively easy access to three different areas for buying higher quality goods and bigger markets to sell crops, livestock, or manufactured goods. Two railroad lines serviced the town after the 1850s, improving travel and enabling shipping to even farther away locations.

Today, Hillsboro is still benefiting from the fruit of the labors of previous generations while continuing their tradition of excellence. The town is still comfortably small but continues to grow and has a bright future. Its citizens are justifiably proud of their town and its history.

One

PUBLIC INSTITUTIONS

After two earlier buildings proved inadequate, the third Highland County Courthouse opened in 1834. It has the distinction of being the longest continuously operating courthouse in Ohio and will celebrate its 190th year in 2024. The 1837-era county jail is visible behind the courthouse; in addition to housing prisoners, it also served as the residence of the sheriff.

The courthouse lawn has long been a gathering place for Hillsboro celebrations. Here, it is filled with a crowd for the 1907 Centennial Homecoming celebrating the town's 100th year. An addition (at left) was made along the back of the courthouse in 1884. This consisted of two wings running perpendicular to the back of the old section. The old jail was torn down to make room for this renovation.

The stone county jail opened in 1895. It was more secure than its two predecessors but had its own issues. For example, passersby could talk with the prisoners through the cell windows along Court Street. Jerry Foley, who did masonry work on the building, ended up being the first to occupy a cell after his booze-filled post-job celebration got out of hand.

The Soldiers' Monument is dedicated to the memory of the soldiers of Highland County who served during the Civil War. A drummer boy beats the "long roll" while the soldier on top scans the horizon for the cause for alarm. The whole monument is 21 feet and 9 inches tall and weighs over 33 tons. It was erected on the courthouse lawn in 1897.

This wintry view from around 1900 shows the courthouse, jail, and Soldiers' Monument. Large-scale snow removal was a difficult proposition in the early years. Instead of clearing roads, people adapted by switching out wheeled carriages for horse-drawn sleighs when the snow reached a sufficient depth.

City Building, Hillsboro, O.

The City Building was erected in 1876 at the southwest corner of Walnut and High Streets. The fire department, village jail, and city offices were on the first floor. The second level held the library and a 1,000-person meeting hall. The clock kept "Hillsboro Time," which ran three and a half minutes behind "Railroad Time." The clock's face could be read from four blocks away, and its chimes were audible four miles away.

The fire engine, hose carriage, and ladder wagon are displayed in front of the City Building some time around 1900. Embarrassingly, despite housing the village's firefighting equipment, the structure burned to the ground in 1949. Fortunately, firemen were able to save the town records, and the library had relocated to the Scott House a short time earlier.

Here, the fire department prepares to parade its steam-powered engine in fine fashion in 1880. The small building at right presently houses Roades Tax and Accounting at 111 West Walnut Street. The firemen had a variety of animal mascots over the years, including a small monkey that stole fruit from stores and was a general nuisance. It was named Eck after temperamental longtime fireman John Reckley.

Greenwood Cemetery was established in 1859, after the town's earliest cemeteries had become full or neglected. Over time, the bodies and tombstones from the old burying grounds were moved to the new cemetery. Hillsboro Cemetery, as it is now more commonly known, originally consisted of 30 acres. It has a number of old-growth trees that shade many of the earliest grave sites.

Recognizing a need for better medical care for Highland County, a group of doctors came together in 1911 to urge the formation of a hospital. By 1914, the former home of William T. Bowers had been converted into the 35-bed Hillsboro Hospital. This facility served the medical needs of the region until 1963, when the current Highland District Hospital was built.

The inmates and officials of the Highland County Children's Home pose on the front lawn around 1900. The children's home was open from 1898 until 1941. It sheltered over 700 needy or orphaned children during this time. Before the children's home opened, there was little assistance for these youngsters; they had to work to support themselves unless a Good Samaritan took them in.

The water-pumping station shown here was built in 1893 near the Clear Creek basin north of town. It was originally able to deliver at least one million gallons per day to the old rocket-shaped water tower. This tower was 135 feet high, 15 feet in diameter, and held 175,000 gallons. Initially, it did not have a cover, and children would climb up to sneak a swim.

The center of population for the United States is the point at which the number of people living to the east and west of the location is the same. The 1870 Census determined the center of population was at the eastern edge of Hillsboro, specifically at the home of Dr. Robert Doak Lilley. A monument was erected on the site in 1970 to commemorate the location. (Photograph by the author.)

In 1816, Josh Woodrow built a large home on the northeast corner of High and Beech Streets. It was soon converted into a fine hotel, the Woodrow House, which the Woodrow family ran for almost 50 years. A series of owners subsequently continued the establishment for another 50 years. It was renamed the Clifton House in 1887. The hotel eventually deteriorated and was closed in 1914.

The Hillsboro Armory was built in 1914 on the site of the former Woodrow/Clifton House. It was the base for Company D, 1st Regiment Infantry of the Ohio National Guard, which was formed in 1899. The first floor of the armory had a 53-by-85-foot drill hall that was also used for dances, meetings, and high school activities such as basketball games.

The Union School was built in 1868 at the corner of Walnut and Elm Streets. Renamed Webster School in 1896, this facility was used for 89 years; in 1957, a replacement Webster was built in a single-story U shape around the old school. The old building was then carefully dismantled, leaving space for a playground.

Various additions were made to Webster School over the years to relieve the continual space issues. Some of these additions are visible in this c. 1915 view of the eastern side of Webster. The poorly built fire escapes were added in 1908; the builders had to come back to repair their work after a piece fell and injured a student.

After the Highland Institute closed in 1889, its building was used to house public high school classes from 1890 through 1896. The old building was declared structurally unsound, which finally forced the town to construct a new school building to be used in conjunction with Webster School. Apparently, the building was considered sound enough to house orphans, as it then served as the children's home until 1940.

Washington School was built at the corner of Beech and East Streets. Opened in 1896, it originally housed the high school, though some other grades were also located there. In the 1950s, Washington was gutted. Its decorative features were removed, and the outer walls were shifted to convert the elaborate Victorian architecture into a modern box of brick and glass. The new Washington School remained in use until 2005.

The Washington School class of 1913 is shown assembled in one of the school's classrooms. From 1898 through 1914, Ohio law only allowed admission into high school to students who could pass the difficult Patterson-Boxwell test after finishing eighth grade. The high school graduation rate was fairly low, even among these elite students. A typical example is the class of 1908, which started with 62 freshmen but ended up having only 22 graduates.

From 1893 to at least 1914, Hillsboro High School had a student cadet corps that trained members with military marching drills, calisthenics, and patriotism. The cadet corps was an optional activity, but members could earn school credit through their involvement. This group of cadets was photographed in 1907 in front of Washington School.

The first football game played in Hillsboro took place at the fairgrounds on November 29, 1894. Hillsboro won 46-8 against a team from Chillicothe, though only three members of the home team had ever seen a game. The *News Herald* described the players in this picture, taken by professional photographer Philip Weyrich, as "posing like crouched lions with their faces turned fiercely toward the foe."

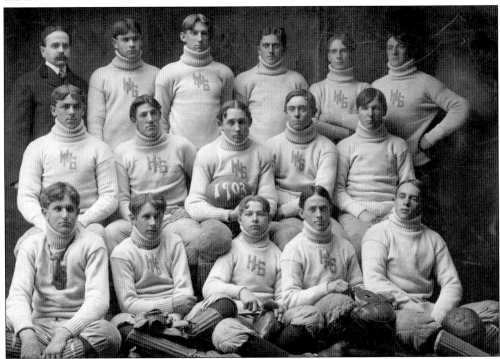

The 1903 Hillsboro High School football team members pose proudly in their team sweaters. Note the primitive metal nose guard around the neck of the player at lower left. Football was popular among students, but adults were concerned about the dangers of the sport. After recent Hillsboro graduate Richard Evans was paralyzed and died playing in a college game, the sport was banned in Hillsboro from 1907 to 1917.

Basketball has been popular among the students of Hillsboro High School for well over a century. Pictured here is the 1904 team, which may have been the school's first. They played a home game against a team from Covington, Kentucky, that the *News Herald* honestly reported as "disgusting to all lovers of clean, honest sport" due to the "rank unfairness of the local referee."

A girls' basketball team existed at Hillsboro High School as early as 1904. The young lady at right was quite an athlete, as she is also included in team photographs from 1905 and 1906. In the 1920s, varsity letters were issued in basketball. However, all intermural girls' sports in Ohio high schools were discontinued in 1940 and were not resumed until 1974.

Baseball was very popular with the young people of Hillsboro, but most of the early teams were associated with the town rather than a school. The first official school team, shown here, came together in 1894, but it did not last. Teams were formed and disbanded over subsequent years depending on student interest.

The 1909 Hillsboro High School track team was especially successful due to Harry Roads (at right in the second row) and Ed Ayres (at center in the first row). This two-man track team placed second overall at the state meet. Both gentlemen won two events while setting new state records, and Ayres also finished second in the broad jump. His jump of 20 feet and 7 inches set a school record that stood for 66 years.

Two

WOMEN'S COLLEGES

For almost 60 years, Hillsboro was home to at least one women's college. This photograph of the Hillsboro Female College class of 1860 was likely taken in 1858. The woman in the center of the first row is teacher Mattie Mather; she had graduated from Oakland Female Seminary in 1856 and stayed on as a teacher for most of the next 30 years.

Rev. Joseph McDowell Mathews was a sickly man who was incapable of speaking above a whisper. Despite his limitations, Reverend Mathews started three institutions of higher learning in Hillsboro and almost single-handedly endowed the town with a reputation for academic excellence. He came to town in 1827 to be the first teacher at Hillsboro Academy. When he found he could not control his male students, he devoted his life to women's education. Mathews founded the Oakland Female Seminary in 1839 in the old Presbyterian church on the triangle between US Route 50 and State Route 124. While Oakland was not the first college in Ohio to allow female students, it may have been the first founded specifically for women. Oakland got a new building and a new name in 1857, becoming Hillsboro Female College. Mathews later had a disagreement with the college board and left to restart Oakland. The Hillsboro Female College continued without him until 1873, when he returned. Poor health forced him to retire in 1877, and he passed away in 1879.

Oakland Female Seminary had strict rules designed to keep girls focused on their studies and isolated from distractions, especially young men. These rules gradually relaxed over the years, but these colleges were not finishing schools or social clubs. The academics were rigorous, and the graduates earned an education equal to that offered in contemporary men's schools.

The Hillsboro Female College was bordered by Main, Oak, and Walnut Streets. It was 90 feet long and 50 feet wide with a flat roof designed for promenading and studying the night sky with a telescope. Students slept in one large room on the third floor, with their sleeping spaces separated by curtains. Classes were held on the first and second levels. The two-story back ell housed the school chapel.

25

When the Methodists started Hillsboro Female College, the Presbyterians got jealous and started their own school, the Highland Institute, in the building that had previously housed Oakland Female Seminary. The institute was run by Emilie Grand-Girard, who had graduated from Oakland and taught there for 14 years. The Highland Institute was much more focused on social events than the other Hillsboro women's colleges, but its academics were still solid. In 1866, a new building was erected to replace the dilapidated 50-year-old church-turned-school. Grand-Girard ran the school for 26 years and continued as a teacher for three more. Poor health forced her to retire in 1888. The institute could not survive without her and closed a year later. The old institute building was then used as the public high school from 1890 to 1896 before housing the children's home for 42 years. It was torn down in 1951 and replaced with a similar-looking two-story building that stored copies of a Cincinnati insurance company's business records so the company could continue operations if its Cincinnati headquarters was hit by an atomic bomb.

Three

THE TEMPERANCE CRUSADE

Hillsboro began to host monthly livestock sales in 1869. While many horses were sold and traded, the event soon degenerated into a weekend of drinking and carousing. The notorious excesses of the attendees exhausted the town and helped set the mood for the 1873–1874 Temperance Crusade. This view of a sale was taken from the center of town and looks down West Main Street.

Dr. Dio Lewis gave a temperance lecture on December 23, 1873, in which he urged the women of Hillsboro to publicly pray, sing hymns, and demand an end to the sale of alcohol. The next morning, the ladies met at the Presbyterian church to launch the Women's Temperance Crusade by marching on the town's pharmacists, one of whom had sold as many as 756 gallons of whiskey during the previous six months.

Though not present at the initial lecture by Dr. Dio Lewis, Eliza Jane Trimble Thompson, the daughter of Gov. Allen Trimble, was elected to be the leader of the crusade. The ladies were sure she would want to be involved, as it was well known that her oldest child, Allen Trimble Thompson, died in 1868 from the effects of alcoholism, and her daughter, Marie Rives, was married to a habitual drunk.

John W. Bales, "Dealer in Pure Wines & Liquors," was located near the later site of the Masonic temple. Bales was arrested for assault and battery for pushing Maria Pickering off the sidewalk in front of his saloon when she blocked his entrance. After two trials, he was eventually declared not guilty.

John W. Bales was an entrepreneur. He started the first billiard hall in town and ran a shoemaking enterprise next to his saloon. His emblem, the "High Wooden Boot," is visible at right. Bales remained defiant before the temperance crusaders. The white sign posted by his saloon door reads: "Twenty Years, or During the War! I Don't Surrender."

Temperance crusaders hold forth in front of North High Street liquor seller Robert Ward in March 1874. Ward was one of the last holdouts along with John W. Bales and Jake Uhrig and pharmacist W.H.H. Dunn. Ward's saloon was considered to be a high-class establishment that was patronized by the socially elite men of Hillsboro. Ward and Bales both managed to survive the crusade and continued selling whiskey to the husbands and sons of the crusaders.

A slightly different view of North High Street in the spring of 1874 shows that the saloons of John Bales and Robert Ward were only separated by three doors. This helps illustrate how concentrated the approximately 20 liquor sellers were around town. Ward's neighbor to the south, J.L. West (right), began his dry goods store in 1873 and ran it for five years.

In January 1874, after the temperance crusaders cowed East Main Street saloon owner Jake Uhrig into selling the contents of his bar, they dragged three barrels of his whiskey into the center of town, smashed them open, and lit them aflame. In the background is the James J. Brown Drug Store, which was picketed by marchers on the first day. Brown had almost immediately signed the pledge to not sell alcohol.

William Henry Harrison Dunn's Palace Drug Store was located near the southeast corner of Main and High Streets. Dunn had recently become the full owner and extensively renovated the store. After he refused to stop selling liquor, the temperance crusaders defiantly put up a "tabernacle" outside his store. Dunn filed an injunction that brought down the tabernacle after only one day, January 31, 1874, but he was soon bankrupted by the crusade.

With her white cap and long black clothes, Eliza Jane "Mother" Thompson became a symbol of the temperance movement for many years. However, there were 70 other women who accompanied her on the first march and 75 others who quickly joined them. These ladies were from the wealthiest families of Hillsboro, and many had received a higher education at one of the local women's colleges. This picture was taken around 1890.

Hillsboro's Temperance Crusade was not the first mass public uprising of women against the evils of alcohol, nor was it very successful long-term, as the Hillsboro liquor trade soon recovered. However, it was the most famous, and it led to the founding of the Women's Christian Temperance Union and, eventually, the 18th Amendment and Prohibition. Perhaps Eliza Jane "Mother" Thompson was pondering some of this as she examined a flower near her back porch in 1900.

Four

CHURCHES

Hillsboro Methodist Church began in 1806 with circuit-riding ministers. In 1810, they built the first church in Hillsboro, which was located on Court Street. In 1815, a larger log church with an octagonal front was built on Walnut Street. It was replaced in 1822 with a brick church with a balcony on three sides. The present sanctuary was finished in 1853 and continues to house the congregation.

Starting in 1896, Hillsboro Methodist Church offered young boys membership in a club called the Epworth Guards. Members pledged to lead lives free from tobacco, intoxicating liquors, and unchaste thoughts or actions. They practiced military marching drills but carried wooden canes in place of guns. This was a short-lived club that lasted only a few years.

In 1845, a priest visiting from Fayetteville found 15 Catholic families living in Hillsboro. He began the process of establishing a parish for the area, and St. Mary's Catholic Church was organized in 1852. The church building was finished the next year. It is shown here in 1890, a decade before it was rebuilt. The first rectory is at right.

Hillsboro's earliest Presbyterian church was located several miles east of town. The second church was built in 1818 at the Y intersection at the east end of town, and a third church was built at the corner of Main and East Streets in 1831. The Crusade Church (pictured) was built at the same site in 1849 and remained in use until 1894.

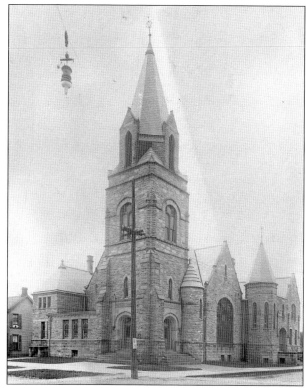

The current First Presbyterian Church of Hillsboro took four years to complete. Finished in 1899, it is a lovely Gothic-style edifice made of Berea sandstone. A series of beautiful stained-glass windows featuring the Last Supper, the Resurrection, and the Ascension are especially striking. The front tower contains the same bell that rang out from the Crusade Church. The $40,000 project was fully funded by generous donations from the congregation.

The First Baptist Church only had 10 congregants when it was formed in 1843. After initially meeting in homes, the congregation built its first church on West Street at what would later become the site of Swonger's Dairy. In 1906, after 60 years, the 149-member congregation moved to its present church at the nearby northwest corner of Walnut and West Streets.

This house, the longtime residence of Dr. Enos Holmes, was located on the northwest corner of Walnut and West Streets before the First Baptist Church was built there. Dr. Holmes was a doctor in Highland County as early as 1838. He moved to Hillsboro in 1856 and practiced there for another 32 years. Dr. Holmes died suddenly while seeing patients at his office in 1888.

St. Mary's Episcopal Church was formed in 1850. After five years, the congregation decided to build a church. It initially planned to build across the street from the newly constructed St. Mary's Catholic Church but decided the corner of High and North Streets was better suited to its needs. A simple church was built, but it became more elaborately decorated as more money was raised. The most notable features are the exquisite stained-glass memorial windows. The arched front door has been painted an eye-catching bright red for many years. An elaborate pipe organ was installed in 1885 in memory of Dr. Edward Rives by his sister, Margaret King, who was heartbroken over his untimely death. This organ still provides music for church services and concerts. One of the rectors of the church, Zebarney Thorne Phillips, went on to become the chaplain for the US Senate and the dean of the National Cathedral.

In 1888, one hundred people came together to found the Hillsboro Church of Christ. Four years later, this church was constructed at the southeast corner of Walnut and West Streets. In 1914, an especially successful revival suddenly added 300 new members to the assembly. To accommodate the increased membership, the church was enlarged to double the seating capacity.

The United Brethren Church had its beginnings in 1818. The congregation met outside town in its earlier years but built a church at the northwest corner of High and South Streets in 1902. This building has housed several other congregations during its existence.

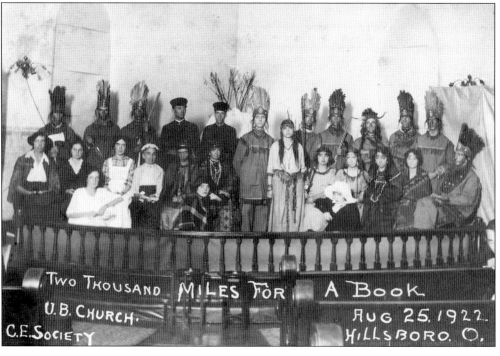

Five

TRANSPORTATION

Here, Bell's foundry owner Charles Elliott Bell drives an elaborate six-seat carriage equipped with headlamps. This would not be a typical vehicle on the streets of Hillsboro. The Bell family had a barn full of carriages and wagons, much as wealthy people today collect fancy cars. Another photograph of the carriage refers to it as the Tally-Ho, which was slang for a fast vehicle.

A fine-looking horse is harnessed to a basic buggy. A buggy is a lightweight carriage that typically has seating for two people and often has a top that can be folded down, as shown here. The horse and buggy are parked in front of the Highland Institute building around 1900. By this time, the Highland Institute had closed, and the building housed the Highland County Children's Home.

Ledger E. "Frog" McConnaughey is shown at the reins of the Lemon & Chaney grocery store delivery wagon in 1921. They are in the alley behind North High Street, and the trees behind the wagon are growing on the future site of Colony Theater. Pete Evans is behind the wagon. McConnaughey later worked as a driver for Hillsboro Ice Delivery from 1925 to 1949 before driving for the Hillsboro Fire Department until 1969.

Usually, horses were used to pull carriages because they are fast and easy to train. However, this happy-looking gentleman has managed to hitch a slightly put-out Hereford bull or steer to haul his rig. Note the corn stalks in the field in the background—corn was cut by hand, and 12 to 15 stalks were tied together to dry to be stored for winter feeding.

A delicate-looking young heifer is hauling these five young ladies as they take a ride in a buggy. According to the back of the photograph, the girls' names are Helen Crampton, Ethel Jones, Hazel Bauer, Olive Martin, and Wilma Eubanks, but there is no indication of which girl is which.

On January 12, 1869, W.B. Kinkead successfully rode the first velocipede, or bicycle, in Hillsboro. His one-block ride on the homemade vehicle was followed by several decades of bicycle mania in Hillsboro. This picture shows the Hillsboro Bicycle Club in August 1896. From left to right are Clyde C. Patton, Helena Brown, Ann Quinn, Berry Matthews, D. Rockhold, Maggie Ferris, A.E. Hough, May Cummings, Charles B. Smith, and Daisy Spargur.

Bicycle races of up to 50 miles were held at the fairgrounds on the horse track and on local roads. This particular race had its starting line in the center of town. The large building in the background is Charles Haynes's Cheap Cash Dry Goods Store. Merchants Bank was built on the site in 1900.

The history of Hillsboro's railroads is a jumble of companies forming, consolidating, going bankrupt, and being bought at bargain prices. Fortunes were made by a few investors, but many more faced financial hardship or ruin when a rail line did not develop as hoped. The first train arrived in Hillsboro on September 22, 1852, on the Hillsboro & Cincinnati line. Cincinnati lawyer Rutherford B. Hayes, who would later serve as the 19th president of the United States, was the main speaker for the opening ceremony. Other railroads that attempted to service—with varying degrees of success—include the Marietta & Cincinnati; Chesapeake & Ohio; Cincinnati, Gallipolis & Pomeroy; Columbus & Maysville; Cincinnati, Portsmouth & Virginia; and Cincinnati, Washington & Baltimore. The situation finally settled by the end of the 19th century, leaving two national lines servicing Hillsboro—the Baltimore & Ohio Southwest and the Norfolk & Western Railway (N&W), which is shown here. The N&W came to town in 1902; its depot was located on West Street, near McDowell Street, across from the present-day Master Feed Mill, and the railroad ran trains through Hillsboro until 1986.

Baltimore & Ohio Southwest acquired a rail line into Hillsboro in 1889. A year later, a modern and elegant passenger depot with a long, covered walkway was built on the north side of West Main Street at the site of the new city park and former Highland Enterprise Lumber Company. In 1937, the depot building was moved across Main Street, where it remains today.

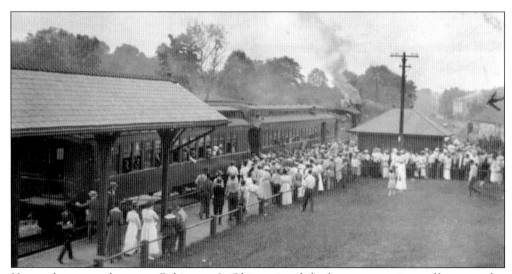

Here, a large crowd greets a Baltimore & Ohio train while the steam engine puffs out smoke. The small building behind the telephone pole is the baggage room. The arrow at right indicates where the Globe Chair Factory varnished and stored its products. A rail spur ran alongside this building for easy loading. The Globe Chair Factory building burned down in 1903, and in 1914, the baggage room also suffered a fire.

A rail spur for Beecher's Quarry passed under a bridge on North High Street near the Catherine Street intersection. This bridge and much of the spur were filled in by 1924, but part of this path can still be seen on the east side of North High Street where tall rocky walls form a narrow channel between houses. A wrought iron fence protects pedestrians from the sudden drop.

Railcars are lined up at the end of the spur in Beecher's Quarry and ready to be filled with limestone. Once the quarry ceased to operate around 1920, the pit was abandoned. Trespassers soon adopted it as an unofficial playground. They camped, ice-skated, and rode bicycles and dirt bikes in the old quarry.

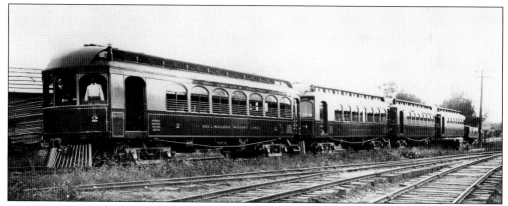

The Cincinnati & Columbus Traction Company (C&C) made its first trip in 1905. This electric railroad ran from Cincinnati to Hillsboro on tracks parallel to present-day US Route 50. A planned expansion to Columbus never came about due to the bankruptcy of the company after 14 years of operation. The C&C was nicknamed the Swing Line because several of the founders had the last name Swing.

The Norfolk & Western Railroad initially refused to let the Cincinnati & Columbus Traction Company cross its tracks, so for two years, passengers had to disembark outside of town and take a horse-drawn wagon the rest of the way. The C&C eventually won a court case that permitted it to cross the N&W's line and complete the route into town, which looped around the courthouse. The C&C's depot (right) was on Court Street.

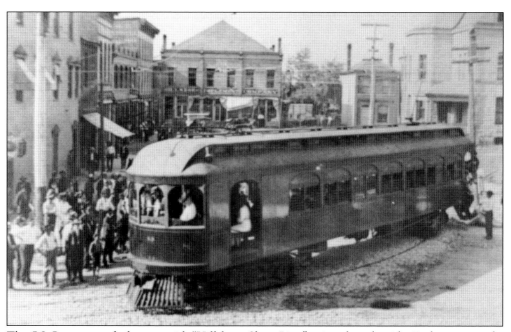

The C&C cars were dark green with "Hillsboro Short Line" painted on the side. Each car was eight feet wide and divided into three sections. The main area, highlighted with green plush seats and mahogany woodwork, seated 38 passengers. A smoking compartment had seating for 16, and the baggage compartment offered 12 second-class seats. Each car had a toilet and hot water.

C&C cars departed Hillsboro for Owensville nine times per day—at 5:25 a.m., 7:30 a.m., 8:25 a.m., 10:30 a.m., 12:30 p.m., 2:30 p.m., 3:30 p.m., 5:30 p.m., and 7:30 p.m. The traction cars were forbidden to travel faster than eight miles per hour within the town limits. As shown here, railroads were not immune to weather-based difficulties. The last run for the C&C was on October 25, 1919, as it could not be made profitable.

Hamer McConnaughey (left) is showing off his 1911 Hudson Roadster to his passenger and boss, Kirby White. It is fortunate the car is carrying a spare tire, as the left rear tire looks to be in rough shape. McConnaughey tragically died at the age of 21 when he drowned at the Point near Cave Road.

In this photograph from 1916, John (left) and Sinai Howard (right) and an unnamed woman enjoy a ride in an immaculately maintained vehicle. Sinai was the live-in superintendent of the Highland County Children's Home from 1899 until her death in 1926. Her daughter-in-law Nellie Blount took over the operation of the home until its closure in 1940.

Two cars competed in a 20-mile race at the Leesburg Fairgrounds on September 5, 1914—*Old Daisy* (left), a Studebaker driven by Lewis Stanley and owned by Hillsboro automobile dealers Ervin & Dragoo, and a Mercer (right) driven by Erk Kerr and owned by Donald McClain from Greenfield. The Mercer won easily, as it was an expensive sports car, while the Studebaker was a stripped-down everyday model.

On March 21, 1919, a pilot had engine trouble and was forced to make an emergency landing in a field to the north of town. This event caused much excitement as townspeople rushed out to investigate the novel technology.

Hillsboro's streets were first paved in 1920. Previous paving initiatives had failed to generate enough support; the *News Herald* declared the 1920 plan to be unwise and impractically expensive and suggested that a sewer system was needed more than paved roads. The arrow at the top points out the Smith/Ayres drugstore on East Main Street. Note that the mortar and pestle has been disassembled for the project.

This is the same location as the previous picture but at a later stage of paving. The nondescript three-story building to the left of the prominent Spargur building was the home of jeweler Jacob Sayler for many years. His son, John Sayler, was an early photographer who was responsible for the pictures of the 1873–1874 temperance crusaders and Hillsboro scenes.

Six

BUSINESS

Upon arriving in Hillsboro in 1858, C.S. Bell bought the Clayton Foundry on the corner of Beech and Railroad Streets. He began by manufacturing stoves but soon diversified the business to include a variety of metal implements for the home, farm, and industry. After a worker dropped a piece of metal that rang like a bell, Bell experimented with various steel alloys until he found one that rang exceptionally well.

Steel alloy bells could be made and sold for a fraction of the cost of brass or bronze bells, and the sound travelled farther, though the tone was considered to be a bit less musical. The bells were popular and sold well. Due to the increased demand, in 1895, a larger foundry was built on a seven-acre plat at the intersection of McDowell and Railroad Streets.

Workers at C.S. Bell's foundry pause to have their photograph taken. Several are holding the tools of their trade, including hand bellows, spud bars, and shovels. The foundry was, for the time, a relatively safe place to work; the first fatal accident was not recorded until 1901, after 30 years of operation.

The C.S. Bell Company sold bells and tools all over the world but was especially successful in South America, where its food grinders and sugarcane mills were popular. This photograph of a worker demonstrating a horse-powered cane mill is an advertisement for the South American market. The sign reads: "Manufactured by the C.S. Bell Co. Hillsboro, Ohio E.U.A. Sold by Isaacs Hermanos Honda, Colombia."

While the C.S. Bell Company made many small, relatively simple items such as coffee grinders, grain mills, and bells, it also manufactured large pieces of complex equipment, such as this industrial-sized sugar and sorghum mill. The foundry offered 200 possible sizes and styles of this type of mill.

Charles Singleton Bell was the founder of the C.S. Bell Company. While he did not attend church or trifle much in politics, he was heavily involved in other civic matters. Bell was the longest-serving school board member in the history of Hillsboro public schools, he built Bell's Opera House to provide the town with culture and entertainment, and he assisted almost every public and semipublic institution in Hillsboro with substantial financial support.

Not much is known about C.S. Bell's wife, Mary Louise Roberts Bell. Unlike Hillsboro's other wealthy society ladies, Mary did not take part in many social activities and was not involved in the Temperance Crusade. She survived her husband by 15 years and lived in the family home with a daughter and three servants until her death in 1920.

Charles Elliott "C.E." Bell was the second generation of Bells to run the foundry. During his tenure, the company concentrated on the manufacture of farm implements, as the bell market was depressed. C.E. led a bit of a wild life and at least once required the services of a good lawyer to get him out of legal trouble. He married Eleanor Beatty Hane, who was almost 30 years his junior.

Charles Beatty Bell and Virginia Bell Thompson Telfair were the children of C.E. and Eleanor Bell. In 1934, 28-year-old Virginia took control of the family's failing company. She stabilized its finances and acquired a government contract to make ship bells for the US Navy during World War II. By 1944, the company had made 26,000 Navy bells. Virginia managed the foundry until 1969, when the Bell family sold the business.

The Smith/Ayres drugstore was open for 171 years and, at one time, was the oldest continually running drugstore in Ohio. It was opened in 1808 by Dr. Jasper Hand, who also served as an army surgeon in the War of 1812. His successor, Dr. Jacob Kirby, ran the pharmacy for over 50 years. William Robinson Smith, Kirby's son-in-law, had the store, then called W.R. Smith and Company, until 1900, when his three sons took over. In 1925, longtime clerk Ed Ayres bought the store and renamed it Ayres Drug Store. After the death of Ayres in 1964, the store continued operating until 1979. The big red mortar and pestle out front has marked the location of the drugstore for close to 150 years. This piece was purchased at the 1876 Centennial Exposition in Philadelphia. It has been taken down only twice—in 1920, when the streets were paved, and in 1964, when a freak wind blew off the top.

Founded in April 1854 by Paul Harsha, the Harsha Monument Company is Hillsboro's longest continually operating business. The Harsha family has operated it for 169 years—or six generations. When this picture was taken around 1880, the business was located at 134 South High Street. It was moved into its current location at 127 West Walnut Street in 1893. (Courtesy of Harsha Monument.)

This was the original Walnut Street home of Harsha Monument. In 1963, the 70-year-old frame building was torn down and replaced with the current concrete block structure. The company is proud of its long history and prominently displays photographs and artifacts from the business's long history in the large front showroom. (Courtesy of Harsha Monument.)

The Hibben Dry Goods store was founded by Samuel Entriken Hibben in 1826 on five lots along the east side of North High Street. This store remained open at the same location for the next 132 years. In 1957, it was declared to be the oldest dry goods store west of the Allegheny Mountains.

Five buildings composed the Hibben store, with the central store at 112 North High Street being the main show room. This is the interior of one of these buildings. An early Hillsboro colloquialism, "As honest as Sam Hibben," highlights the integrity of the store's founder. Hibben was an early abolitionist, supported temperance, was a leader of the Presbyterian church, and served in the Ohio State Senate for one term.

Joseph Matthew Hibben took over the store and continued his father Samuel's tradition of excellence, honesty, and passion for civic matters. Joseph's son, Samuel Galloway Hibben, was a lighting engineer of national importance. He designed the lighting effects for the Statue of Liberty, Washington Monument, World's Fairs, and Carlsbad Caverns, among other large projects. Another grandson of Samuel Hibben, John Grier Hibben, served as president of Princeton University from 1912 to 1932.

After Joseph Hibben retired, the store stayed in his family, but the owner elected to live elsewhere and trusted Frank Zane (center) to manage the dry goods store. Zane performed this duty for 50 years, from 1908 until the store's final closure in April 1958. Frank's sister, Kathryn Zane Granger (right), also worked in the store for many years as a cashier.

The Kibler & Herron building on South High Street was built in 1879. This store had its origins in the 1834 hardware store of Joseph Kibler. The "Sign of the Red Anvil" was its identifying image, which can be seen on the roof. The business was later renamed the Hillsboro Hardware Company, then Fairley Hardware. It closed in 1987 after over 150 continuous years of operation.

The windows of Joseph Stabler's 5 and 10 Cent Store are full of souvenirs commemorating the 1907 Centennial Homecoming celebration. Just a year later, this store was completely destroyed by a fire. Stabler then built a new store on North High Street. In 1928, the devastating Murphy-Benham fire just barely spared the second Stabler building.

The Union Grocery Store was formed in 1900 when three established grocers decided to go into business together. The store was located on West Main Street, one door east of the Parker Hotel. By 1904, only Friend F. Stevens remained. He partnered with Joseph Garvey and continued the grocery until 1920, when Stevens retired and Garvey went into politics.

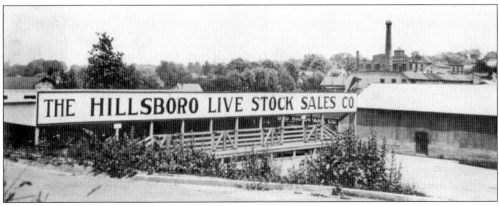

Located at the corner of Main and Elm Streets, the Hillsboro Live Stock Sales Company gave farmers in the area a good market to sell their cattle, pigs, and sheep. This company became the Union Stockyards, which relocated out of town, partly due to the complaints of modern city dwellers with sensitive noses. In the background is the smokestack of the Hillsboro Light and Power Company.

Fred Zane set up his tannery on the north side of East Main Street soon after he arrived in town in 1854. He spent the next 45 years buying pelts, tanning hides, and selling leather products. In 1899, Zane unexpectedly died from tetanus after a nail in his shoe slightly injured his toe.

The Enterprise Planing Mill originated as Utman & Jeans Company in 1873. Originally located near the Baltimore & Ohio station, the company moved to its new location at North West Street in 1884. It later merged with Highland Lumber to form Highland Enterprise Lumber Company, which closed in 2010. The Enterprise building on West Street is still in good condition, although it has not been used for commerce for many years.

This is the office of Dr. John D. McBride, who claimed to have delivered 4,000 babies during his 48 years of practice. He was walking into a maternity call when his car rolled forward, knocked him down, and ran over him. Dr. McBride tended to his patient before seeking help for his broken leg and internal trauma. Complications from these injuries resulted in his death a week later.

The 1911 Model Restaurant was a short-lived side enterprise associated with the popular Model Bakery on West Main Street. The restaurant was not profitable and was soon converted into a pool hall. A second Model Bakery was opened a few years later in the same location by a new owner. It was more successful and remained open into the 1940s. The sidewalk advertisement touts a 25¢ chicken dinner.

Bowles Bookstore (near the center of this c. 1920 photograph) was a Hillsboro tradition from 1852 until 1948. The tangle of wood frames in front of the buildings were supports for awnings that helped shield businesses from the sun's heat. The diagonal line that looks like a railing behind the cars and carriages is the power supply for the Cincinnati & Columbus Traction Car Company and is suspended above the road.

Charles Granger is working at the first chair in the Opera House Barber Shop around 1920. Manning the second chair is Walter Tedrick, who worked as a barber in Hillsboro for almost 50 years. The young man in the back is Patsy Green, who worked as a bootblack for many years. Tragically, Green was murdered in 1935; his killer was put to death in the electric chair for the crime.

The Lemon & Kesler Blacksmith shop is shown in 1907. This business was at 111 South West Street at this time but moved to Walnut Street two years later. The *News Herald* declared "Rip" Lemon to be the leading blacksmith in Hillsboro in 1900. In his younger years, Lemon was a popular player on the town's baseball team.

Charlie Long's blacksmith shop is decorated for the 1907 centennial. Blacksmiths were essential in early Hillsboro. They made nails, tools, and wagon wheel rims, and they repaired many household and industrial items. The best-known job of the blacksmith was the shoeing of horses. These horseshoes had to be custom fit to each horse's foot. The job required great strength and creativity and was hot, hard, and dangerous work.

A lady tries on a new hat at Olive Berryman's hat shop on East Main Street around 1900. Owners of millinery shops offered customers a selection of hats and bonnets that were usually handmade at the establishment. Many of the millinery stores in Hillsboro were owned and operated by female proprietors.

The J.W. Rogers & Company Grocery, located on West Main Street, sports two very large bunches of bananas hanging in the window on the right. The business on the right is a bowling alley, likely associated with the Parker House. Rogers sold his store in early 1908 and later became the owner and manager of the Adams County Mineral Springs Hotel.

Seven

A Walk around Town

Since 1966, the Highland House has served as the headquarters of the Highland County Historical Society. It was built around 1845 for use as the home of Peter Ayres and was converted into a hotel in 1882. The widowed Kate Doorley and her daughter, June, managed the hotel from 1903 until 1964. They made the Highland House locally famous for its fine meals, especially the Sunday dinners.

These cattle are being driven up East Main Street around 1900. The dark three-story building in the center is Spargur Dry Goods. In 1865, the Spargur brothers, John, Henry, and Joseph, opened a store in association with Samuel Hibben; they went independent in 1871 and moved to their new building in 1887. Between them, the three brothers had a total of 40 children, so it is fortunate their business was successful.

The large pocket watch–shaped clock at right was the well-known emblem of watchmaker and jeweler Jacob Sayler, who was located on the north side of East Main Street at the time this picture was taken. Sayler ran his store in various locations around town for almost 70 years. He acquired the clock for the City Building in 1876 and spent the rest of his life overseeing its operation, maintenance, and repairs.

A lone wagon makes its way up East Main Street on a miserable rainy day. No information could be located regarding the Tharp Square Deal Grocery (left), though there are several advertisements for the Cooper's Department Store (right) in 1913 newspapers. The small sign on the telephone pole recommending paint is posted in front of Smith's Drug Store.

The southeast corner of Main and High Streets is called the Johnson Corner in honor of its first owner, merchant Benjamin H. Johnson. The Evans & Ferris banking house moved to this corner in 1868. In 1879, this building was erected. A year later, the bank reorganized and was renamed Merchants Bank. Note that Jacob Sayler and his clock were located on South High Street when this picture was taken.

The south side of West Main Street seems to have been the most important commercial street in Hillsboro and was certainly the most photographed. Note the carbon arc street lamp hanging over the intersection. These gas-powered lights were introduced in 1875. They were hard to keep lit, especially on windy nights. Electricity came to the town in 1893.

The Sam Free Store (at left) originated in 1854, when Mayer Free started a men's clothing store. His son Sam took over in 1891 and moved into the old Smith Corner. The store closed in 1939, after Sam's death. In this picture, a bandwagon is in the intersection and the horses on the right are hauling either water or oil to spray down the earthen streets to reduce the dust.

This photograph by John Sayler shows businesses on the south side of West Main Street in 1874. From left to right, they are T.A. Walker (clothing), J.J. Brown's Drugstore, the Citizens' Bank, Amen & Miller (grocery and hardware), Bumgarner & Elliott (dry goods), William T. Bower's Bakery & Confectionary and residence, J. Sayler (jeweler), N. Rockhold & Son (hardware), Henry Strain & Company (grocery), and I.P. Strauss & Brothers (clothing).

For those who could not read, stores would try to link their establishment with a particular image. One example is the mortar and pestle in front of Ayres Drugs. In this 1874 picture, Jacob Sayler, in the small building in the center, has a small pocket watch over his doorway. The Rockhold Hardware store next door claimed the "Sign of the Circular Saw," which is arched above its entryway.

In 1873, the businesses along this stretch of West Main Street included, from left to right: I.P. Strauss & Bro. (clothing), Hiestand & Ayres (household/glassware), Morrow Dry Goods, R.R. Waddell, John Bowles Bookstore, Charles Utman Furniture, and C. Kinkead (photographer). Note the skylight in the roof and larger window (at right) that provide better light for taking pictures.

The businesses shown in the 1880s on this part of West Main Street are, from left to right: Isaac A. Feibel's clothing store; Kaufmann's Wholesale Liquor & Cigars; R.R. Waddell, jeweler; A.Z. Foulk's Photography; Barrere's Drug Store; and a small part of the Parker Hotel. The flag in the center of the Strauss building has 38 stars, and it was used from 1876 through 1889.

This is basically the same view as the one in the previous picture, but it shows the section of West Main Street about 30 years later, during the 1907 centennial. The large building in the center, containing Kaufmann & Baer, the Model Bakery, and the Parker House Billiard Hall, burned down in the Famous Store fire in 1936. The Parker House Hotel is at right. After Isaac Feibel's death in 1892, his sons, Louis, Julius, and Michael, took over the business and opened a branch store in Columbus. Both Feibel Brothers stores closed in 1924. Isaac Kaufmann's brother-in-law, Aaron Baer, joined him in the liquor business in 1880. Later, when Hillsboro voted to restrict the sale of alcohol, they became pharmacists. Charles Gorman bought their closeout stock in May 1906. The day of the sale, Gorman was arrested when several barrels and many bottles of various spirits were found in his new store. He eventually paid a $200 fine because of the contraband.

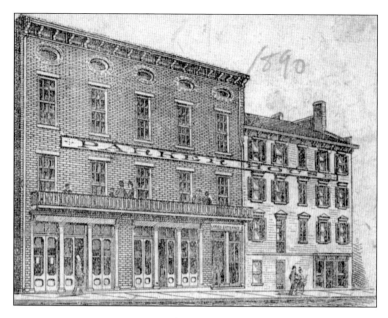

The Knox Tavern, a small log cabin, was the second building constructed in Hillsboro after its 1807 founding. Early legal proceedings were held at this location. After multiple additions, the tavern became a hotel in 1826, first called the Eagle Hotel, then the Ellicott House. By 1893, it received its final name, the Parker House. The final structure had 40 rooms and was known for its excellent meals.

The Pigtail Done Tavern was a feature of the Parker House Hotel. Guests were called to their meals each night by the ringing of a dinner bell. It became a tradition to call out jokingly "Pigtail done!" when it was heard, giving the establishment its unusual nickname. The name later became attached to the bar that was in the Parker House.

As West Main Street continued beyond West Street, businesses were replaced by residences. At left is the Fallon House, later called the Hill City Hotel. The Hillsboro Female College building is visible in the distance toward the right. This photograph helps to convey how large the college building was and how it dominated the view to the west of Hillsboro.

The street is being paved at the northwest corner of Main and West Streets, where the Republican headquarters is now located. The Baltimore & Ohio railroad depot was located behind these buildings. The businesses pictured here include, from left to right, the Jefferson House, a garage offering expert auto repairs, a place selling Gold Medal flour, and a coal dealer.

McKeehan-Hiestand, a wholesale grocery store, was located on the northeast corner of Main and West Streets from 1892 until 1941. The company supplied groceries to many small stores in rural southern Ohio. The *Hillsboro Dispatch* newspaper shared the grocery's building. The two young ladies celebrating the 1907 centennial in the carriage are Mozelle Trop (left) and Nellie Brunner (right).

Philip Kramer opened the Kramer House (the two buildings with awnings over the windows) in 1870. The hotel had 36 rooms, a dining room, a bar (off limits to women), and a billiard parlor. It acted as a party venue, meeting room, and funeral home. Jacob Shack operated a livery stable at the rear of the hotel. In 1895, a room at the Kramer cost $2 per day.

The location where Glascock & Bro. Hardware once stood at the corner of West Main and Short Streets (now Governor Foraker Place) is now the site of a Domino's Pizza. The house in the background was the home of Judge James Sloane in 1874, when this picture was taken. It was later the site of the Hillsboro Implement Company.

Some young gentlemen pause in their labors to discuss the news of the day in this c. 1874 image. In the background at left is the jail/residence of the sheriff, and at right is the back of the courthouse. This is the jail that the Rainsboro-born Western outlaw Robert McKimee escaped from after being arrested for crimes he had committed in the Black Hills area.

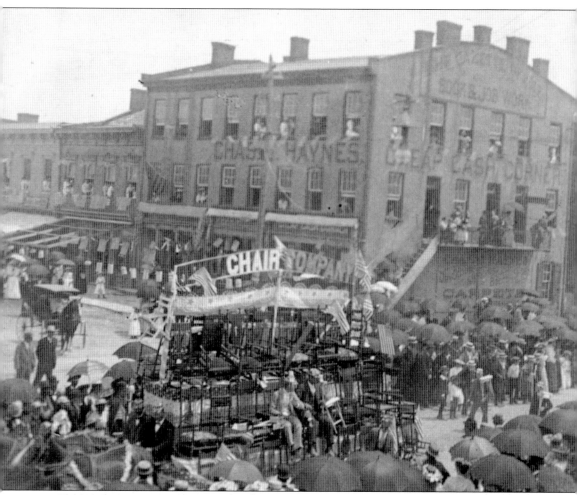

The northeast corner of Main and High Streets was originally known as the Fallis Corner due to Daniel J. Fallis and the Cheap Cash Corner store he built there in 1847. In 1872, two years before this picture was taken, Asa Haynes started selling clothing, dry goods, notions, and carpet at the location. By 1888, his son, Charles, was running the business. The balcony along the East Main Street wall of the Haynes building was known as Loafer's Roost. As indicated by the name, it was considered by many citizens to be a nuisance. The Ohio Chair Company can be seen parading its wares through the street—this was a short-lived enterprise that ran from 1891 to 1894.

Seybert & L.T. Isamenn (center right) bought Dr. Hugh Fullerton's East Main Street drugstore in 1872. Their trademark was the "Sign of the Blue Front" or just "Blue Front." They willingly signed the temperance crusaders' pledge when challenged on the first day of marching. Isamenn retired and sold his share back to Dr. Fullerton in 1874. This store, named Seybert & Company, was in business for several decades.

Looking up East Main Street, the 1900 Merchants Bank building is at the corner. This angle shows that the top of the bank was actually a decorative facade. The two-story, light-colored building with two windows (right) housed the jewelry store of Eli W. Muntz. In addition to selling jewelry, Muntz was a wood carver and repaired bicycles, watches, and guns. At the far right, someone is offering "Cash for Cream."

This crowd at the October 1908 Hillsboro Expo fills East Main Street near the empty stage where the baby show and other events were held in front of the W.R. Smith Drug Store. The E.L. Harris Grocery, visible at far right, was in operation from about 1900 through around 1909.

This view of the far end of East Main Street was taken about 10 years after the previous photograph. The building next to Smith Drugs is called The Oak: Pocket Billiards and Lunch Room. No information could be found regarding this establishment, so it can be assumed it was a short-lived enterprise.

To capture this view from 1910 looking north up High Street, the photographer had to stand in the middle of the road near the intersection with Walnut Street. Note that the streetlight is powered by electricity (compared to the previous gas-powered arc light). A banner across the street at the center of town advertises a Hillsboro Chautauqua.

This picture was taken during the summer of 1896 and shows the new Bell's Opera House. The Gus Sun Minstrel Show is parading to build interest for a coming show. At some point, the smaller prominence and flagpole on the roof of Bell's was removed. At the far left is the City Building.

Before Bell's Opera House was built, the western side of South High Street was occupied by a row of shanties known as Rat's Row. These dilapidated buildings had been an embarrassment for the town since the 1875 Smith Corner fire. On the morning of April 4, 1894, the demolition of Rat's Row began. Seven months later, Bell's Opera House held its opening night.

Bell's Opera House was next door to the Smith building on the southwest corner of Main and High Streets. Here, the Smith Corner (later called the Sam Free Corner) is decorated for the 1907 Centennial Homecoming. Farmers & Traders National Bank was organized in 1893. It moved into the corner building in 1925 and was located there under various names until 2018.

The Trimble building, on the corner of Court and North High Streets, housed numerous businesses from 1812 until 1909, when demolition was being done on both sides in preparation for a new structure, which caused the Trimble building to collapse unexpectedly. The occupant of the building was out for lunch, so no one was injured.

Based on the presence of the Trimble building (left) and the Stabler/Orpheum building (right), this North High Street scene is from 1909. The Stabler building was steam-heated and had extensive electrical lighting throughout. It also had an elaborate soda fountain that became a favorite place for ladies to meet for a visit.

The Bell Block replaced the Trimble building in 1912. This structure was owned by Joseph G. Bell, who rented the office space to a variety of enterprises. In 1920, the Murphy-Benham Hardware Company took over the main room in the building, and most locals then referred to it as the Murphy-Benham building. On an eight-degree January night in 1928, a fire broke out in the basement. Attendees of a dance on the third floor had to scamper to evacuate, but amazingly, no one was hurt in what would prove to be the worst fire in the town's history. The Bell Block, which also contained the post office, was completely destroyed along with the Palace Theater, Stevenson's Jewelry, the old Traction building, and Dr. J.D. McBride's office. The extreme cold made fighting the fire especially difficult, and photographs from the night show neighboring structures such as the Soldiers' Monument covered with thick icicles from the effort.

Taken from the northwest corner of Beech and High Streets and looking south toward the center of town, this photograph shows the entire east side of North High Street in the 1880s. At left is the still-active Masonic temple. The smaller three-story building partway up the block is the current site of SOS Office Supply.

This winter scene on North High Street is from February 5, 1892. Garrett Brothers Drug Store, at the second telephone pole from the right, is marked by the dark, rectangular "Drugs" sign. This business was started in 1840 by James M. Brown and had several different names and owners until it closed in 1947, at which time it was called Highland Drugs.

A horse-drawn sleigh traverses the east side of North High Street in this March 1917 photograph. The second building from the left is Bowles's Bookstore, and Garrett & Ayres is visible near the horse's head. The two buildings at right housed the E.H. McClure Ironclad Clothing Company and Miller's Drug Store.

The two locations of Merchants Bank have confused Hillsboro historians for years. From 1866 until 1900, it was located on the southeast corner of Main and High Streets (Johnson Corner). It then moved to its new building, shown here decorated for the 1907 centennial, on the northeast corner of Main and High Streets (Fallis/Haynes Corner), where it remains today.

This busy scene from the 1907 Centennial Homecoming celebration shows attendees watching a demonstration of a troupe that would be appearing at the Bell's Opera House. The north side of East Main Street is visible at left. There are five different businesses in the Hillsboro Bank building: Hillsboro Bank, J.C. Shaw Shoes, Hollingsworth & Walker Shoes, and the law offices of Charles Collins and George Gardner.

The John Armstrong Smith house was located on South High Street directly opposite from Bell's Opera House. The temperance crusaders would go inside the home to warm up and have tea between bouts of prayer while protesting the recalcitrant liquor seller W.H.H. Dunn. This photograph was taken just before the house was torn down in 1896.

After the Smith house was demolished, the Glenn Building (with the triangular peaked roof) and the Stabler's 5 and 10 took its place. The white building with four windows to the left was demolished in 1968, when Hillsboro Bank expanded its building. This photograph shows the Hillsboro Post Office's mail carriers with their horses and delivery vehicles, including a bicycle.

This row of buildings is on the east side of South High Street after the alley. The Hill City Grocery started in 1904 and was managed by D.D. Hiestand. Around this time, other businesses along this section of street included Trop's Millinery, Capital Tire Company, J.C. Shaw Shoes, O.S. Lemon Monuments, Nickeson's Meat Market, Dr. William Hoyt, a candy shop, and Posey Zink's grocery.

Court Street remained a mostly residential street until around 1890. The Waddell Building (left, with the two peaks) was erected in 1892 and set in front of the preexisting building on the right. There were complaints of it darkening the post office considerably. The C&C Traction Company office and depot was in the partially blocked three-story square building.

The Hillsboro Implement Company was on Court Street near the intersection with Short Street. The company was formed in 1899 by James Williams and Joseph G. Bell, who would later build the Bell Block. Bell was the store's full owner by 1902. The company was bought in 1920 by Nesbit and Blount and moved into the Masonic temple building.

Here, a parade traverses Short Street some time in the 1910s. The last building on the street, closest to Hillsboro Implement, was Michael F. Carroll's carriage factory, which began in the 1870s. Carroll's sons joined the business in 1900 and quickly adapted to the changing times, offering automotive repairs and selling cars for the Dodge Brothers Motor Company. The back of the jail and traction rails are at the right.

This photograph shows the buildings on the northern end of Short Street. The one-story building in the center of this picture has a large coffeepot on the roof as an advertisement. The renovated Carroll building (at right) housed the Royal Blue Market from the 1960s through 1974. This area was razed in the 1970s for the construction of the county administration building.

Eight

ENTERTAINMENT
AND BIG EVENTS

In 1907, Hillsboro threw a three-day Centennial Homecoming celebration to commemorate the 100th anniversary of the founding of the town. Over 20,000 people attended the highly successful event. It led to several other well-attended festivals and expos over the next few years. This smartly decorated welcome wagon can be seen in several pictures from the centennial.

One of the most popular events of the October 1908 Hillsboro Exposition was the baby show. It was held on a stage in front of Smith Drug Store next to the mortar and pestle. Numerous spectators endangered their lives by climbing to the tops of nearby buildings and utility poles to watch the proceedings. Similar daredevil observers can be seen in other pictures of Hillsboro's large street celebrations.

The winner of the baby show is at the center of this photograph, with the bottom of its dress marked with a cross. Hopefully, the person holding this child is a sibling or cousin, as she appears to be very young. The mother sitting to the right of the winner appears to vigorously disagree with the judges' decision.

Whatever attraction was being offered by the Sam Free building during the 1908 Hillsboro Exposition must have been especially interesting, as seven individuals risked their lives for a better view. There are two men sitting atop the telephone pole at right and five men on the telephone pole at left.

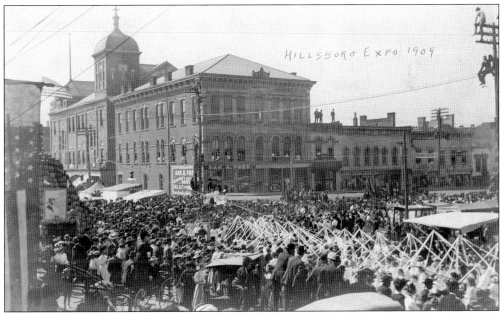

A huge crowd filled the center of town to watch a parade of Hillsboro public school students. Four men are perched on the telephone pole to the right, with one sitting fully on the wire, and two men are standing at the top of the pole at the Smith/Sam Free Corner with several others lower down the pole.

The Pumpkin Palace photograph from the 1909 Hillsboro Expo combines Hillsboro's love of huge festivals, imaginatively stacked produce, and climbing dangerously high to get a better view (note the man crouched at the top of the telephone pole by Sam Free's store). The Ferris wheel in the background looks almost as hazardous as climbing to the top of a telephone pole.

Another view of the Pumpkin Palace shows that people could walk inside. During the Hillsboro Expo, Coca-Cola, ice cream cones, and pumpkin pies were sold out of the Pumpkin Palace. The message on the sign (with the farmer with the corncob pipe) is a boring economic statement bragging about how much money crops were sold for in 1909, to which the farmer replies "Gosh all Hemlock!"

Prized cattle paraded past the courthouse during one of the street fairs. The one-horned bull at right, named Prince of Perth, is being led by a Mr. Ware. They are followed by Marion Meyers with Nominator. Meyers achieved a doctorate degree in agricultural science and became a pioneer in developing hybrid seed corn. His Meyers Hybrid Corn Company became the largest private producer of seed stock in the United States.

The Corn Palace was built for the 1913 Street Exposition. The walls were covered with yellow corn ears and had decorative highlights of white corn on the corners. The roof and flagpole support were made of fodder stalks. The goal of the expo was to highlight Highland County's best agricultural products from that year, but it also exhibited local accomplishments in sewing, baking, gardening, and students' work from the public schools.

Parades were a mainstay of local street fairs. This entry by the C.F. Whisler lumber mill is a battleship made from oak veneer. In 1914, Whisler had a recreation hall built for the young people of Hillsboro, though he died before it was completed. In 1920, Whisler's widow, Mary, donated $10,000 to save the failing Hillsboro Hospital, with the provision that the facility be nonprofit and open to everyone.

This parade entry advertised the Austin & Horst real estate and insurance company. Prior to the founding of this firm, Frank Austin had been a buyer and shipper of leaf tobacco. Otto Horst had been a lawyer since 1893, and he continued his legal practice in addition to running his real estate and insurance business.

With seating for 1,000, the C.S. Bell-owned Bell's Opera House was an impressive facility for a town that had only around 4,000 inhabitants. Stage shows were performed at the location into the 1930s. Silent films were shown as early as 1901, and the opera house became a fully equipped movie theater in 1923. Bell's Opera House closed around 1939, after the Colony Theater opened.

This rare interior view of Bell's Opera House is from late 1922 and shows a crowd of actors on the main stage. Dramatic companies would come to town once a year to offer a week of shows for locals. The play *Uncle Tom's Cabin* was a Hillsboro favorite, especially due to the presence of the George Beecher family, who lived on the eastern edge of town.

In 1909, the owners of the Fair Store created a theater next to their business, which was located in the rebuilt Stabler 5 and 10 building on High Street. At first it was called the Fair Theatorium, but in 1912, the name was changed to the Forum. A 5¢ matinee was offered every Saturday at 2:00 p.m. as well as an evening show The Forum changed management multiple times before it closed permanently in 1951.

One Forum owner was arrested in 1914 for the crime of operating his theater on a Sunday. Another manager, Homer Barnes, shocked the community when, on March 18, 1919, he viciously murdered his wife, Charlotte. Barnes was judged to be insane and sent to an asylum, but he was soon declared to be cured and released. Barnes's successor, George Rea, shown here, ran the Forum starting in 1919.

George and Mary Rea stand under an ad for the 1918 D.W. Griffith movie *The Great Love*, starring Lillian Gish. Mary Rea played a pipe organ to provide the musical accompaniment for the silent films that were shown at the Forum and for various musical entertainments that were occasionally offered at the theater. George sometimes joined in, playing the xylophone and drums.

The Orpheum Theater opened in 1908 on North High Street in the new Stabler building. The shorts advertised in this picture include *Broncho Billy's Mistake*, *A Tenderfoot Hero*, and *Rounding Up the Counterfeiters*—all of these were released in 1913. The Orpheum closed on September 16, 1923. Owner Newt Chaney is pictured here.

Chautauquas were part of a nationwide adult education lecture circuit at which speakers presented programs on a variety of topics, including literature, science, morals, and politics. There were also entertainments, including musical selections, magicians, and storytellers. It was somewhat similar to vaudeville but was considered to be a higher-class form of entertainment, at least initially. The Hillsboro Chautauqua was active from 1908 through 1931.

Various Chautauquas were held on the Washington and Webster school grounds and on a field at the end of South High Street near Muntz Street, roughly where Ponderosa is located today. Jacob Sayler, the longtime Hillsboro jeweler, is in attendance at this program. He is in the front row at far left wearing a black jacket and white vest.

The 13th Regimental Band was formed in 1878 by merging the Nobel Light Guard Band and the Hillsboro Cornet Band, which had been entertaining Hillsboro since the end of the Civil War. The 13th Regimental Band was the preeminent local band of its era and played at many community gatherings. Both the 13th Regiment and its band were disbanded by order of the Ohio governor in 1899.

In response to the town being without a band, 18 young men organized the Hillsboro Military Band. Its first concert was held on May 16, 1901, and it was advertised as being in the center of town, directly under the electric light. A temporary bandstand was erected for the event, but it was hoped that the regular stand would be returned to its spot on the courthouse lawn.

From the 1870s through the 1910s, John Robinson's Circus came to Hillsboro every spring to put on a show. One of the highlights was a troop of four elephants, including the very popular Tilly. When a circus came to a town, it was traditional for the company to do a big parade through the streets when it arrived and lead people to the site of the show.

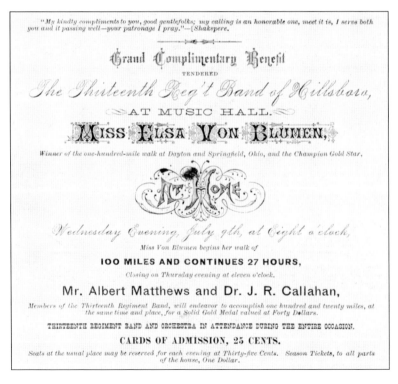

On July 9, 1879, competitive walker Elsa Von Blumen challenged Albert Mathews and Dr. J.R. Callahan to walk 120 miles (60 miles each) faster than she could walk 100 miles. She finished her 100 miles in 22:20:00. Dr. Callahan finished his 60 miles in 11:05:00. Albert Mathews's parents made him stop after 21 miles, much like how they later made him divorce his first wife.

On December 12, 1872, the Episcopal church held an unusual fundraiser at the Music Hall—"An Exhibition of Madame Jarley's Wax Works." There were no actual wax statues involved. Instead, about 50 townspeople dressed as various literary characters and acted out a short scene while "Madame Jarley," played by 18-year-old Julius Pangburn, provided humorous commentary. The exhibition netted $85 for the church.

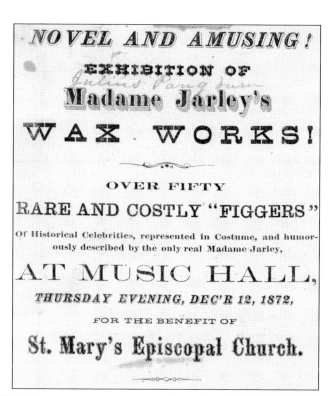

The Boy Scouts are shown preparing to celebrate Memorial Day in the 1920s. The first Boy Scout troop in Hillsboro was organized in 1911, though it was not registered with the national organization until later. The first official troop was organized in 1917. The two troops were unified in 1920. Milton Caniff, creator of the comic strips *Terry and the Pirates* and *Steve Canyon*, is at far right.

Highland Lodge No. 38 was organized in 1817. Benjamin H. Johnson, the namesake of the Johnson Corner, was the first member. When he died in 1854, he bequeathed $10,000 and the lot on the southeast corner of High and Beech Streets to the lodge. Due to some legal complications, it took until 1876 for the Hillsboro Temple to be built.

In 1917, to celebrate the 100th year of the Masonic temple, it was renovated and rededicated. The renovation took about a year, from August 1916 through October 1917. At that time, Campbell's Department Store and the *Hillsboro Dispatch* newspaper office were located in the two store locations on the first floor.

Outings to the Rocky Fork Caves (later called the Seven Caves) at the far eastern edge of the county offered a popular leisure activity for Hillsboro citizens seeking a cool spot. The large, open Dancing Cave was the site of many dances and picnics, while the Marble Cave provided children with pearl-like stalactites as playthings.

The Hillsboro Female College building had a flat roof that was designed for promenading and stargazing with a telescope. The view of Hillsboro and the surrounding area from this roof was reported to be spectacular. It was claimed that one could see for a distance of 15 to 20 miles on a clear day. At left, the town electric plant is belching out thick, black smoke.

The morning of September 16, 1881, was a gloomy, rainy day. Businesses had been suspended, and schools were closed. At 9:00 a.m., every church bell rang out, calling 2,000 citizens to a small pavilion in front of the courthouse to mourn the recently assassinated Pres. James Garfield. Note that at this time, there was an iron fence around the courthouse lawn.

William Jennings Bryan was a nationally known lawyer, orator, and Democratic politician. Despite rainy weather, he drew a large crowd when he appeared in Hillsboro in October 1919. He was in town to make a speech in support of the soon-to-be-enacted Eighteenth Amendment, which ushered in Prohibition. Merchants Bank is at the back.

Cries of "Fire!" rang out on the night of Sunday, May 2, 1875. The Smith Corner was alight, and a powerful wind threatened to spread the fire through the whole town. A 20-year-old hand-powered fire engine, a few firemen, and hundreds of citizens with buckets fought the flames for three hours and heroically saved the town.

At noon on May 18, 1894, a fire was discovered at Hillsboro College. Firemen were close to beating back the flames and saving the main part of the building, but at a critical point, the well the fire engine was pumping from abruptly went dry. As the firemen hurried to access a different water source, the fire raged out of control, and the whole building was lost.

Eight businesses were destroyed or damaged and 14 horses died in the 1908 Barrett Livery fire on South High Street. The livery was completely consumed, while the Stabler building next door was gutted. Across the street, every window at Bell's Opera House cracked from the heat. There was almost no water pressure in the fire plugs, as the water tower was only half full, and the power station was shut down for the night. The town was saved through the efforts of one solitary fire engine pump and the firemen and people of the town who came out en masse to help. One firefighter worked for hours on top of a seemingly empty tank, but when it started melting and the top fell apart, he discovered it contained 60 gallons of gasoline. In this photograph, workers are repairing the telephone lines while the fire is still smoldering.

Nine

MILITARY

This picture of Civil War veterans was taken in 1895 at the Hillsboro Fairgrounds racetrack grandstand. Note the man holding a crutch in the front row, the man near the center of the second row with an eyepatch, and the man in the center of the sixth row who is holding his cane aloft.

In 1862, before they left for service in the Civil War, brothers Capt. David Mitchell Barrett and Richard Cyrus Barrett posed for this portrait. Though they were residents of Paint Township, they were in the 89th Regiment with many soldiers from Hillsboro. Almost the entire regiment was captured at the Battle of Chickamauga in 1863, including the Barrett brothers. They were sent to Andersonville, a notoriously harsh Confederate prisoner of war camp. Many in the 89th Regiment died in the camp, while others were killed in the explosion of the riverboat *Sultana* after their release. David managed to escape Andersonville in early 1865 and travelled 250 miles looking for the Union lines. Exhaustion and sickness forced him to surrender a second time. Both brothers survived their ordeal and enjoyed long lives. David owned Barretts Mill until his death in 1909 and was active in politics. While in Andersonville, Cyrus was stricken with "an insidious disease" from which he never fully recovered. He returned to the farm where he had been born and lived a quiet existence.

In 1898, signing up for the Spanish-American War was seen as promise of a grand adventure by many young men of Hillsboro. This group of recruits is shown with a proud older man with a flag, most likely a Civil War veteran. A large banquet was held in honor of the new troops the evening before they left to officially report for duty.

The Spanish-American War only lasted for four months, and most of the soldiers from Hillsboro travelled only as far as this camp in Tampa, Florida. While they did not experience combat, they still did not have an easy time. The summer heat, humidity, and voracious insects took a heavy toll on the health of the unacclimated Ohioans. One debilitated soldier died just hours after his return to Hillsboro.

This Spanish cannon was appropriated from Cuba in 1898. A celebration was held on July 4, 1899, to welcome the trophy, but enthusiasm soon waned. Bums and barflies loitered around it when it was on the courthouse lawn, and students used it as an ashtray and trash can when it was moved to Washington School. The cannon was lost when it was donated to a World War II scrap drive.

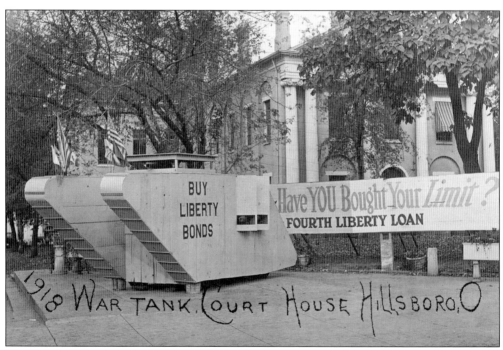

The C.S. Bell Company built this wooden tank to promote to sale of Liberty Bonds for World War I. The citizens of Hillsboro were highly supportive of the effort, which is acknowledged on a plaque mounted to the south wall of the courthouse proclaiming the town's success in meeting its bond sales quota.

A group of young men observes the movements of a small tank on Evans Field at the bottom of the hill behind Washington School. Evans Field was later donated to the school for a playground. It was named in honor of Richard Evans, a popular graduate of the high school who died in 1907 while playing a college football game.

News of the end of World War I reached Hillsboro by telephone from Cincinnati. A large crowd met the next traction car to snap up copies of newspapers detailing the armistice. Hillsboro blossomed with flags, and a parade of hundreds marched through town, led by the workers from Bell's foundry, who banged on scrap metal with their tools. A band appeared, and everyone sang victory songs.

An effigy of Kaiser Wilhelm was paraded through town with a sign proclaiming, "We got the Kaiser." This manikin was hung on the telephone wires at the center of town, shot repeatedly, taken down and kicked by small boys, and finally set on fire. Merchants Bank is in the background.

This picture of the armistice celebration is from a photograph album from the Harold and Susan Henry estate. It is labeled, "Kaiser Bill hung to telephone wire. Nov. 11th, 1918. Big parade when peace was declared." It looks as if a man at far right has recently fired a shot at the "Kaiser" from a rifle.

Ten

MISCELLANEOUS CITIZENS

In 1838, at the age of 18, Dr. David Noble came alone to Ohio from Ireland with nothing to his name. During the Civil War, he served as first surgeon of the 60th Ohio Volunteer Infantry. After his military service, he established a medical practice in Hillsboro. He was also an unusually astute businessman who founded a private lending bank. Dr. Noble personally financed Hillsboro's Noble Light Guard National Guard unit.

Galaxy Pub. Co. Philadª

Cyrus Newby received his legal education in the office of Ulric Sloane. He was admitted to the bar in 1876, then spent 26 years as the judge of the Court of Common Pleas from 1892 to 1918. He was well respected for his impartiality, and his decisions were rarely overturned upon higher review. Newby practiced law for 52 years, right up until his death.

J. Milton Boyd (right) was born in 1817 at what later became the site of the Masonic temple. At 90 years of age, he was the oldest native-born citizen alive at the time of the 1907 Centennial Homecoming. He amazed everyone with his ability to remember the names and personal details of all the former townspeople who came to enjoy the celebration.

Joseph Jefferson McDowell came to Hillsboro in 1824. He went into politics and served in both the Ohio House and Senate. He was also the commander of the Ohio Militia, where he earned the rank of major general. He then returned to Hillsboro to practice law. McDowell returned to politics when he was elected to the US Congress, serving in the 28th and 29th Congresses from 1844 to 1847.

Alphonso Hart was born in Trumbull County. He became a lawyer at the age of 21, served as an Ohio state senator, and was elected lieutenant governor of Ohio (a position he held from 1873 to 1875). In 1878, he came to Hillsboro when he married Anna Ferris Evans, the wealthy young widow of Foreman Evans, a founder of Merchants Bank. Hart was elected to one term in the US House of Representatives.

Dr. Robert Windsor Pratt grew up in Dodsonville on the family farm. He became interested in learning medicine and spent many hours studying the subject in borrowed textbooks. After graduating from medical school in 1900, he started a practice in Pricetown, then moved into Hillsboro. Dr. Pratt worked in medicine for over 50 years. He and his wife, Verda Mae Gossett, were married for 55 years.

Hugh Fullerton, shown at lower right as a member of Hillsboro's first football team, became a sports reporter who was syndicated in over 40 newspapers. He learned that the White Sox were going to throw the 1919 World Series, so he and pitching great Christy Mathewson watched the series and kept track of all the suspicious plays. Fullerton then wrote an article that exposed the infamous Black Sox scandal.

Margaret Sayler (right) was married to jeweler Jacob Sayler. She was heavily involved in the temperance movement, though she was not a first-day marcher. She was the first woman in Hillsboro to reach the age of 100, and she retained her faculties until her death two months and eight days later. Her daughter, Emma Detwiler, and her three granddaughters, Irene, Margaret, and Frances, were renowned Hillsboro artists.

Charles H. Collins was a successful attorney in Hillsboro for 40 years, from the time of his arrival in 1864 until his death in 1904. Collins was a frequent international traveler and a prolific writer, especially of poetry, which was described as virile, with no effeminacy or weak sentimentality. This portrait was taken in 1857, when he was 25 years old.

Galaxy Pub. Co Philad^a

Allen Trimble was arguably the most important figure in Hillsboro history. The Trimble family came to Highland County in 1805 with 20-year-old eldest son Allen acting as head of the family. He became clerk of courts in 1809, then advanced to county recorder. He was elected to the Ohio House in 1816, and a year later, he moved into the Ohio State Senate. He served four terms in the state senate and was speaker of that body for eight years. Because of this position, Trimble served as governor of Ohio for one year in 1820, when the current governor was appointed to the US Senate after the death of the incumbent, who happened to be Allen's brother, William. Allen won election as governor in 1826 and ultimately served two terms. During his time as governor, Trimble helped establish the first public school system in Ohio, set up the first turnpikes and canals in the state, and advocated for establishing Ohio colleges. He was well known for his personal integrity, his promotion of temperance, and his strong Christian faith.

Roy Asa Haynes published and edited the *Hillsboro Dispatch* newspaper from 1908 until 1920. He was appointed to be the first federal Prohibition commissioner by presidents Warren G. Harding and Calvin Coolidge, who put him in charge of enforcing the ban on the manufacture, movement, and sale of alcoholic beverages. Haynes served in this office from 1920 through 1925. His grandmother Ada Haynes had been one of the original temperance crusaders.

George Buckingham Beecher was a member of a nationally famous family of intellectuals, writers, ministers, and activists that included his aunt, Harriet Beecher Stowe, author of *Uncle Tom's Cabin*, and his uncle, Henry Ward Beecher, the controversial head of the first megachurch in the United States. However, George was satisfied with a quiet life of anonymity in Hillsboro and did not chase fame and controversy like some members of his extended family.

Dr. Elizabeth Edmonston came to Hillsboro in 1911. She was a short, stout woman who wore men's hats, coats, and cuff links with a skirt and blouse, carried a man's cane, kept her hair short, smoked cigars, and swore with vigor. Despite her unconventional ways, Dr. Edmonston was accepted into Hillsboro society and considered to be an excellent doctor.

Helen Strain demonstrates her horse-riding prowess at the 1923 Highland County Fair. The message on the back of this photograph states that Helen was "one of the nicest girls that ever lived in Hillsboro. Everyone loved her." Helen graduated high school in 1924. She married Elmer "Shorty" Vogel in 1926 and passed away in 1975.

Frank W. Armstrong served three years in a cavalry unit during the Civil War. He then married into the Trimble family. Blessed with a prodigious memory, Armstrong was a classical scholar and an excellent conversationalist. After he died at the famous Battle Creek Sanitarium, the owner, Dr. John Harvey Kellogg, reported, "I would often stay with him hours when it should have been minutes, owing to the charms of his conversation."

Six fashionable young society ladies show off their elaborate feathered hats and fancy furs in this group picture. They are, from left to right, Mary Fullerton, Rosetta Feibel, Margaret Mackerly, Mary Evans, Nell Nelson, and a Miss Mahan. Feibel was the valedictorian of the Hillsboro High School class of 1893.

Marie Diviess Rives was the daughter of James and Eliza Jane Thompson. She graduated from the Hillsboro Female College in 1866, completing both the English and musical courses. She later served as president of the alumni association. She married Dr. Edward Rives in 1870 but suffered much embarrassment due to his issues with alcohol.

Shown here when she was 25 years old, Mary McArthur Thompson Tuttle was the youngest daughter of James and Eliza Jane Thompson. She graduated from Hillsboro Female College one year after her sister Marie. Following graduation, Mary went to Europe to pursue further education. She married Prof. Herbert Tuttle, who encouraged her academic interests. Mary was a noted lecturer, author, and artist.

When the Civil War broke out, Hillsboro lawyer William O. Collins was serving in the Ohio State Senate. He was commissioned as a colonel and raised a cavalry unit from the men of Highland County. Instead of being sent to fight the Confederate army, in 1862, Colonel Collins and his troops were sent to the Nebraska Territory to protect the Overland Trail. Collins brought his 17-year-old son, Caspar, with him on this journey. Catherine Collins, shown here in her later years, made a dangerous journey to visit her husband and son at the command station in Fort Laramie. When he turned 18, Caspar enlisted in the cavalry under a different commander. He was killed during the Battle of Platte Bridge Station on July 26, 1865, while trying to rescue a wagon train. His heroic stand was not forgotten by the settlers in the area. When a town was founded near the site of the battle, it was named in his honor, though his name was misspelled, and Casper is now the capital of Wyoming. Fort Collins, Colorado, was named to honor Caspar's father.

In 1923, to commemorate the 50th anniversary of the Temperance Crusade, seven of the surviving marchers posed in front of the Presbyterian church. From left to right are Lavinia Dill, Lallie Ferris, Elizabeth West, Sarah Doggett, Margaret Stevens, Josephine Kibler, and Emma Detwiler. The ladies took pleasure in noting that none of the "grog shop" owners who contested them were still alive.

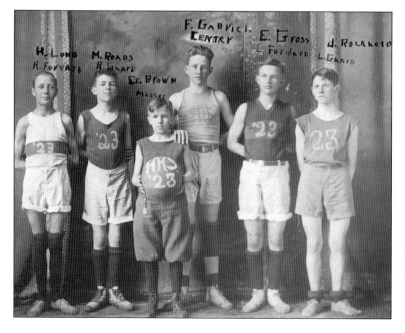

Joe Rockhold (right) is shown as a member of Hillsboro High School's freshman basketball team in 1920. After working in radio after World War II, Rockhold found fame as the title character of *The Uncle Orrie Show*, an unscripted children's television program that aired live each weekday at 4:00 p.m. in the Dayton market. The show ran from 1955 through 1968.

ABOUT THE HIGHLAND COUNTY HISTORICAL SOCIETY

The Highland County Historical Society was formed in 1965 after community leaders realized that Hillsboro's history was in danger of slipping away due to a lack of preservation. The following year, the Highland House building at 151 East Main Street was purchased by the organization to serve as a headquarters for the society and museum of Highland County artifacts. For nearly 60 years, the society has encouraged community involvement in the preservation, education, and promotion of Highland County history and genealogy for the benefit of all people for present and future generations. Because of the support of its members and the generosity and goodwill of those who live in the area, the Highland County Historical Society will continue its preservation efforts for many years to come. Anyone interested in becoming a member or learning more about Hillsboro or Highland County history is encouraged to check out the society's web site at hchsohio.weebly.com.

Discover Thousands of Local History Books
Featuring Millions of Vintage Images

Arcadia Publishing, the leading local history publisher in the United States, is committed to making history accessible and meaningful through publishing books that celebrate and preserve the heritage of America's people and places.

Find more books like this at
www.arcadiapublishing.com

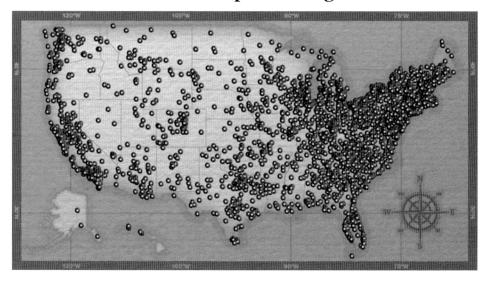

Search for your hometown history, your old stomping grounds, and even your favorite sports team.

Consistent with our mission to preserve history on a local level, this book was printed in South Carolina on American-made paper and manufactured entirely in the United States. Products carrying the accredited Forest Stewardship Council (FSC) label are printed on 100 percent FSC-certified paper.

MADE IN THE USA